3D Dot-to-Dot CITIES

3D Dot-to-Dot CITIES

SHANE MADDEN

THUNDER BAY
P·R·E·S·S

San Diego, California

Thunder Bay Press

An imprint of Printers Row Publishing Group

10350 Barnes Canyon Road, Suite 100, San Diego, CA 92121

www.thunderbaybooks.com

Thunder Bay Press

Publisher: Peter Norton

Publishing Team: Lori Asbury, Ana Parker, Kathryn Chipinka, Aaron Guzman

Editorial Team: JoAnn Padgett, Melinda Allman, Traci Douglas

Production Team: Jonathan Lopes, Rusty von Dyl

This book was designed, conceived, and produced by
Quantum Books Ltd
6 Blundell Street
London, N7 9BH
United Kingdom

Publisher: Kerry Enzor

Managing Editor: Julia Shone

Senior Editor: Philippa Wilkinson

Design: Ginny Zeal

Production Manager: Zarni Win

ISBN: 978-1-62686-880-9

Printed in China by RR Donnelley

21 20 19 18 17 1 2 3 4 5

CONTENTS

Introduction

Pick up your pen—three pens, in fact—and rise to the challenge of working the classic dot-to-dot technique in three dimensions. In this book you will find thirty diverse urban scenes at which to try your hand. Simply join the dots, pop on the 3D glasses, and watch the scene you've created leap into three dimensions before your eyes. You'll be amazed every time.

DRAW IT, COLOR IT, FRAME IT

At the back of this book you will find useful thumbnail pictures of all the completed drawings so that you can easily select the city scene you want to draw. These diverse scenes, with their bridges and skyscrapers, endless rooftops and busy streets, are perfect subjects for this spectacular 3D treatment. Take your pick from landmark buildings, dramatic cityscapes, and sculptural monuments, inspired by metropolises from around the globe. Then grab your pens and get started. All of the pages are blank on the reverse side, which means you can remove and frame your work when you're done.

Remove and frame your completed 3D scenes.

GOING DOTTY

Each image has an average of 800 dots to put your concentration to the test. Once you get started, you'll get into a rhythm, simply moving from one dot to the next, to join ever more of them as you work toward the final image. Turn to page 9 for some helpful tips on how to complete these fiendish puzzles.

Turn to pages 77—79 to find finished thumbnails for each of the puzzles in the book. You can use these to help select which city scene you want to try next, or if you need some guidance to complete the puzzle.

The benefits of 3D dot-to-dot

Dot-to-dot puzzles offer a great way to turn your mind away from the daily stresses of life. You can take time out, relax, and simply focus on moving from one dot to the next. Take the opportunity to switch off from the distractions of every day life and embrace the single-mindedness that these challenges demand.

3D dot-to-dot also provides a mental workout. The moment you start, you become totally focused on finding the next dot, then the next, and so on. You'll be surprised how absorbing the exercise is. But there are more benefits to your mental health than improved concentration. Over time, and with more practice, you will improve your mental agility and attention span, and will generally be more focused at a task in hand, no matter what it is.

How to Use This Book

Put your concentration to the test with one of the thirty dot-to-dot puzzles in this book. Before you get started read through the information on the following pages to get the best out of your design.

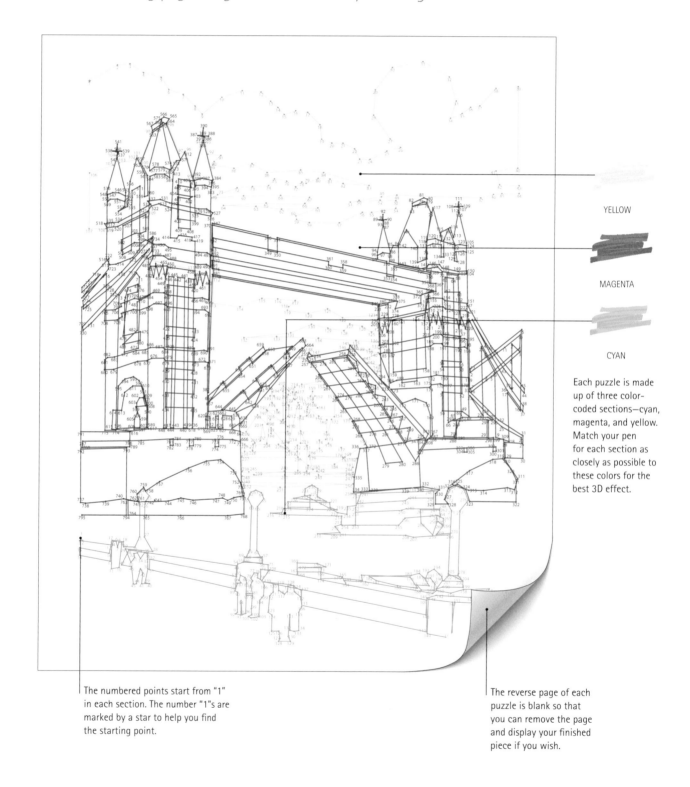

YELLOW

MAGENTA

CYAN

Each puzzle is made up of three color-coded sections—cyan, magenta, and yellow. Match your pen for each section as closely as possible to these colors for the best 3D effect.

The numbered points start from "1" in each section. The number "1"s are marked by a star to help you find the starting point.

The reverse page of each puzzle is blank so that you can remove the page and display your finished piece if you wish.

JOINING THE DOTS

All the illustrations in this book are drawn in three color-coded sections. The dots are organized in such a way that the yellow dots make up the background to the image, the magenta dots build on the mid-ground, and the cyan dots create the foreground. It is essential that you adhere to these three separate colors in order for the 3D effect to work properly (see page 10).

Each of the three colors starts with a star labeled "1" and progresses chronologically to the end dot (numbers vary). There are often as many as 400 dots per color. It makes sense to join all of the dots in one color before progressing to the next, and it is best to start with the background (yellow), then progress to the mid-ground (magenta), and finish with the foreground (cyan).

You will find that you have your own preferred method for approaching the challenges but here are some tips for tackling these extreme dot-to-dots:

- The puzzles have been designed to be completed from background to foreground. Start by joining the yellow dots, then magenta, and finally cyan.

- You may find it helpful to use a ruler to join the dots, particularly for those that are farther apart. This will also help to keep your lines sharp in busy areas.

- Sometimes the next number may be quite far from its predecessor. Follow the pattern to see in which direction the next point should appear.

- Each of the dot-to-dots in this book has been designed to form a detailed illustration. There will be places where your lines cross over lines that you have previously drawn in order to create the detail in the image.

- If you find you struggle with the more detailed areas, you may wish to use a magnifying glass to help.

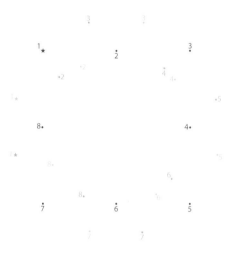

Test pens for each of the three colors using this simple dot-to-dot puzzle. You will need to be able to draw fine lines to maintain the detail of the image.

WHICH MEDIUM TO USE

For drawing the cityscape's outline, it is best to use a fine-nibbed felt-tip or roller ball pen in each of the three basic colors. You need to be able to keep your lines crisp in those areas where the dots are close together. You can experiment with different types of pen, but we recommend using Staedtler triplus fineliner, 0.3 mm, and Stabilo Point 88, fine 0.4 mm pens, which are readily available online and in good craft stores. Try to keep the colors as close to the basic yellow, magenta, and cyan as possible, as bright, vibrant colors work best to create the 3D effect. You can use the color swatches shown here as a guide to match your pen colors and the simple dot-to-dot above to test your chosen pens.

Match your colors

Working With Color

It may be that you wish to color in your finished dot-to-dot drawing. In order to do this without reducing the 3D effect, you'll need to bear in mind how the ChromaDepth® 3D technology works. The glasses make things appear 3D because the lenses register different colors at varying depths of vision. This means that, when coloring in, you need to follow the CMY (Cyan, Magenta, Yellow) color model.

The RGB model

ChromaDepth technology can also work on a black background using the RGB model. In this instance, the glasses read blue as the color farthest away, green as the mid-ground, and red as the foreground. If you opt for this model, remember to color the background black first. This really intensifies the 3D nature of the image when viewed through the ChromaDepth glasses. Then, simply change the color of the pens you use for drawing the initial outline, swapping yellow for blue, magenta for green, and cyan for red. If adding more colors, the warmest colors work best in the foreground and grow progressively cooler as they regress into the background. So, if starting with red as your foreground color, you would work through orange, yellow, green, and purple before finishing with blue in the background.

THE CMY MODEL

On a white background, as in this book, the glasses read yellow as the color farthest away, then magenta as the mid-ground, and cyan as the foreground. Use the colors in a different order, and you will lose the 3D effect. When coloring an image, it is therefore important that any shadows or highlights that you add to increase the 3D effect (see pages 11–13) are made in tones of the same color as the outline. You can use whatever medium you like for coloring—felt-tip pens, crayons, colored pencils. Pencils are especially good if you want to vary the tone and depth of shading to intensify the 3D effect.

INTRODUCING MORE COLORS

If you are feeling adventurous, you can add more colors to your image, but you need to adhere to the warm/cool color spectrum. The warmest colors should be at the center of the image, with mid-warm colors in the background and cool in the foreground. Working from the foreground, therefore, you would start with cyan and progress through violet to magenta, then from magenta you would work through orange to yellow. All of this may take a little trial and error. It may be a good idea to practice a few color ranges on simple 3D shapes first to find the best results.

3D Effects

To emphasize the 3D effect of your image when seen through the ChromaDepth glasses you can try the following techniques when coloring your finished puzzle:

- Consider leaving a narrow outline around each of the main objects in a picture. A narrow band of white background around an image (black if you are using the RGB model) can make an object stand out more.

- Use cross-hatching and shading to emphasize the shape of something, particularly if it has rounded edges.

- Decide which direction the light is coming from and make a few areas darker or pick out one or two highlights.

- Add shadows in those areas where one element stands in front of another.

- Use brighter tones for objects in the foreground and make tones grow progressively darker as you approach the background.

Mid-Warm

Warm

Cool

COMPLETED OUTLINE

Once you have joined the three sections of dots in the puzzle, a dynamic urban
scene will unfold in front of you. When viewed through the ChromaDepth glasses
the artwork will leap into 3D.

For precise lines, use
a ruler to join dots
that are far apart.

Take your time to complete
the more complex sections
of each design—when
you step back from the
dots you will see that
you have just picked out
the towering spire of
a skyscraper or a busy
shopper.

Match the three colors as closely
as possible to cyan, magenta,
and yellow for your outlines
(see page 9).

TAKE IT FURTHER

If there isn't challenge enough in completing these extreme puzzles, take your dot-to-dot to the next level by adding color to your finished piece to enhance the 3D effects.

For each section use tones within the range of cyan, magenta, and yellow to build on the 3D effect.

Experiment with shading and darker and lighter tones to create a sense of depth within each layer of the image.

Narrow outlines of white around main objects can help to make them jump out more.

The Dot-to-Dots

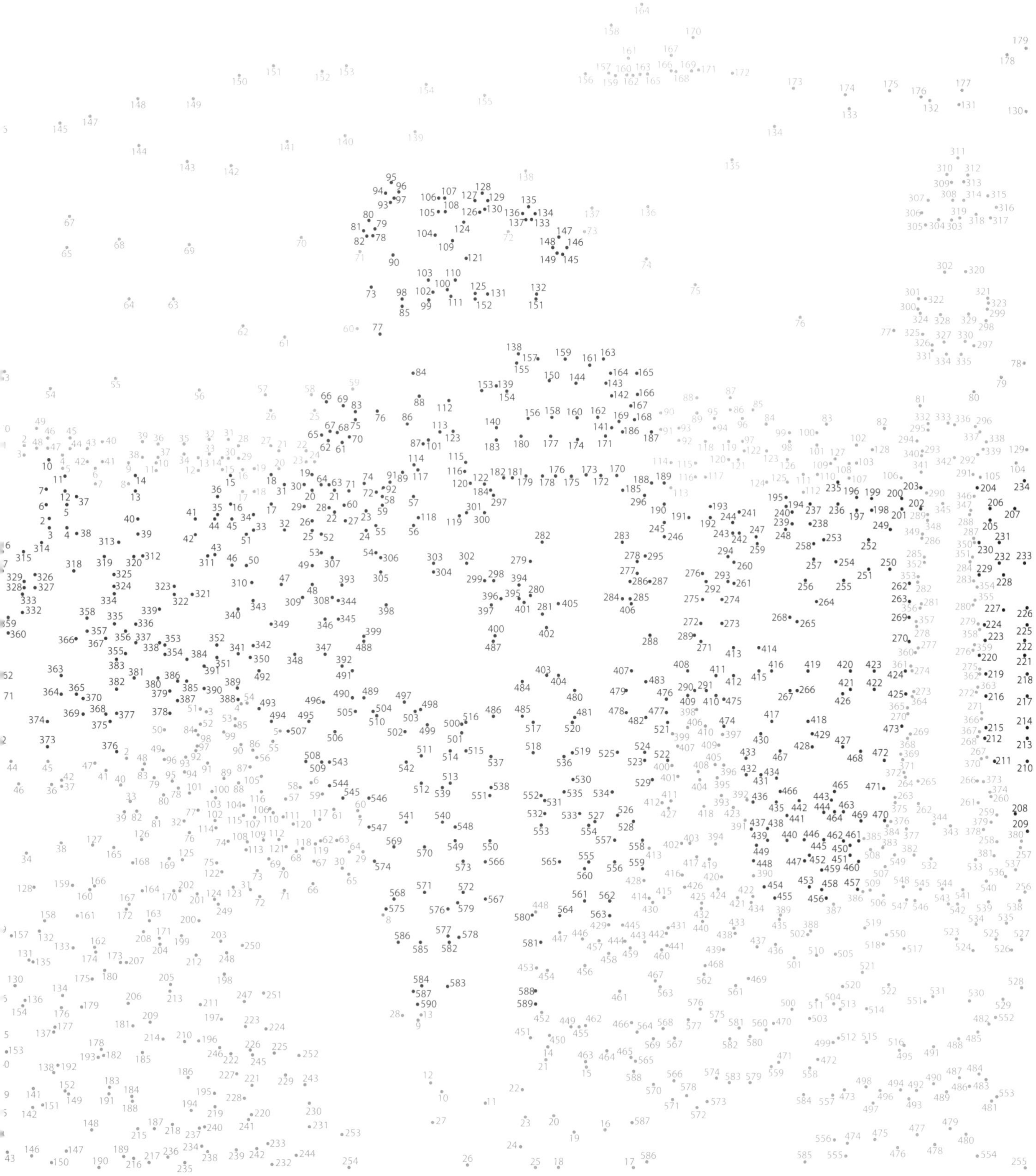

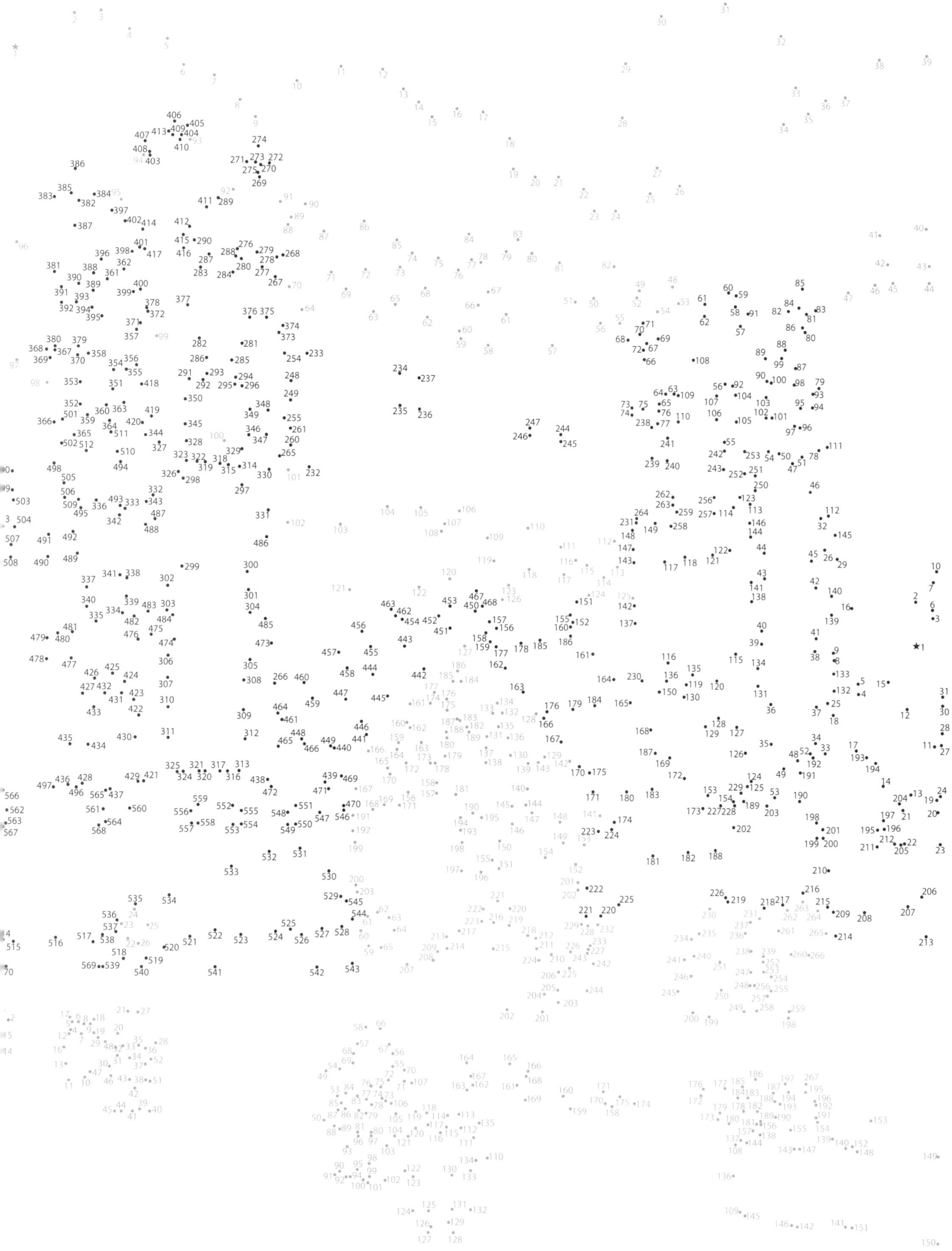

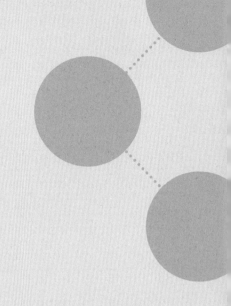

Dot-to-Dot Index

Use the thumbnail images on the following pages to select the puzzle you want to start with, or for guidance if you get stuck.

SKYSCRAPERS
page 17

ON THE BEACH FRONT:
RIO DE JANEIRO
page 19

ANCIENT CITIES:
ROME
page 21

CANAL LIVING:
AMSTERDAM
page 23

SIGNS AND LINES
page 25

HARBOR SIDE:
SYDNEY
page 27

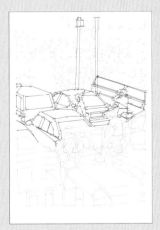

TRAFFIC JAM: DELHI
page 29

GAUDÍ ROOFTOPS:
BARCELONA
page 31

FARMERS' MARKET
page 33

CROSSING THE
WATER: LONDON
page 35

LOOK EAST:
ISTANBUL
page 37

CITY SHOPPING
page 39

COMMUTER BELT
page 41

URBAN PARK:
NEW YORK
page 43

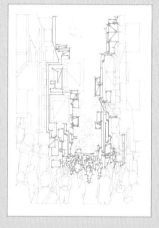

CONSUMER CULTURE:
TOKYO
page 45

OLD AND NEW
page 47

SCENE IN A BAZAAR
page 49

SPIRES AND TURRETS:
MOSCOW
page 51

BUILDING WORKS
page 53

BY THE SEA:
DUBROVNIK
page 55

APARTMENT LIVING
page 57

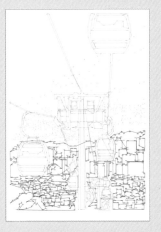

CABLE CARS: LA PAZ
page 59

CAFÉ CULTURE:
PARIS
page 61

DOWN THE ROAD:
SEOUL
page 63

SUBURBAN LIFE
page 65

HIGH STREET
page 67

TRAIN STATION:
BERLIN
page 69

GROWING CITIES:
KUALA LUMPUR
page 71

CITY CYCLING
page 73

LITTLE MERMAID:
COPENHAGEN
page 75

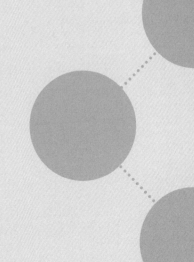

Acknowledgments

Quantum Books would like to thank the following for supplying images for inclusion in this book:

SHUTTERSTOCK.COM
Gearstd, page 11
Mialima, page 9
nevodka, pages 10–11
schab, page 8 right
sumkinn, page 7
vendor, page 11 right

Thanks to the following for their help in making this book:

Our talented illustrator, Shane Madden, for bringing this concept to life and creating such amazing puzzles. It has been great fun exploring the world of 3D Dot-to-Dot with you.

Thanks to Emma Frith Suttey for her expert checking of all the dot-to-dot designs and endless enthusiasm for the project.

Thanks also to Emma Harverson, Nicky Hill, Rachel Malig, Hope Mason, Jade Pallister, Anna Southgate, and Amber Williams for their editorial work; and to Ginny Zeal and Jason Anscomb for their design work and cover design.